FAVORITE NOVENAS TO THE SAINTS

Arranged for Private Prayer on the Feasts of the Saints

•

With a Short Helpful Meditation Before Each Novena

By

REV. LAWRENCE G. LOVASIK, S.V.D.

Divine Word Missionary

Illustrated in Color

CATHOLIC BOOK PUBLISHING CO.
New York

NIHIL OBSTAT: James T. O'Connor, S.T.D.
Censor Librorum

IMPRIMATUR: ✠ Patrick J. Sheridan, D.D.
Vicar General, Archdiocese of New York

The Nihil Obstat and Imprimatur are official declarations that a book or pamphlet is free of doctrinal or moral error. No implication is contained therein that those who have granted the Nihil Obstat and Imprimatur agree with the contents, opinions or statements expressed.

(T-58)

Printed in the U.S.A.

FOREWORD

A NOVENA means nine days of public or private prayer for some special occasion or intention. Its origin goes back to the nine days that the disciples and Mary spent together in prayer between the Ascension and Pentecost Sunday. Over the centuries many novenas have been highly indulgenced by the Church.

To make a novena means to persevere in prayer asking for some favor over a period of nine days in succession or nine weeks. It means fulfilling our Lord's teaching that we must continue praying and never lose confidence. This confidence is based on our Lord's words: "Ask and you will receive; seek and you will find; knock and it will be opened to you. For whoever asks receives; whoever seeks finds; whoever knocks is admitted" (Lk 11:9-10).

Saints are those who distinguish themselves by heroic virtue during life and whom the Church honors as Saints either by her ordinary universal teaching authority or by a solemn definition called canonization. The Church's official recognition of sanctity implies that the persons are now in heavenly glory, that they may be publicly invoked everywhere, and that their virtues during life or Martyr's death is a witness and example to the Christian faithful.

The Church honors the Saints who are already with the Lord in heaven because they inspire us by the heroic example of their lives and intercede for us with God.

Because of our union with Christ we are united with all those who share His life in the larger family of God, the Communion of Saints. We on earth, members of the Church Militant, still fighting the good fight as soldiers of Christ, still journeying on our way to our Father's house, are helped by the prayers and encouragement of the victorious and blessed members of the family, the Church Triumphant in heaven. We honor the Saints and endeavor to imitate the example of their virtuous lives.

We manifest the love and unity that are ours in the Communion of Saints also by praying to the Saints in heaven as our patrons and intercessors with God. Not only is their intercession with God very powerful because of the love they have shown Him on earth, but we also share in their merits gained by their heroic life.

Try to talk with God during your novena. Absolute sincerity is most important. And as you grow in daily reflection and prayer, you will find yourself talking to God with much the same ease as you would converse with a close friend.

Use your own words in this simple, intimate chat with God, and they will gradually become your own personal, individual way of prayer. You will find that the Holy Spirit is enlightening your mind and strengthening your will to do God's Will.

Father Lawrence G. Lovasik, S.V.D

CONTENTS

— MARCH —

SAINT JOHN OF GOD

(March 8)

Patron of Heart Patients

MEDITATION

JOHN was born in Portugal in 1495. He was a shepherd-boy until he was twenty-two years of age. For eighteen years he was a soldier in many parts of Europe. Even though he led a wild life, he loved the poor and the suffering.

John was over forty years old when he left the army in order to make up for his sins. He went back to Spain and rented a house. In it he gathered all the sick, the poor, and the homeless of the town of Granada. Often carrying them there on his own back, he washed them and dressed their sores, and begged food for them. He brought many sinners back to God.

Kind people began to help him in his work. The Order that he founded grew. It became known as the Hospitaller Order of Saint John of God. His motto was: "Labor without stopping; do all the good works you can while you still have the time."

After saving a man from drowning, John became very ill. On March 8, 1550, the nurses found him kneeling before a crucifix, his face resting on the feet of Jesus. The cause of his illness was overexhaustion. He died of a failing heart and is therefore honored as the patron of heart patients.

The feast of Saint John of God is celebrated on March 8.

THE WORD OF GOD

"This . . . is the fasting that I desire: share your bread with the hungry, shelter the needy and the homeless; clothe the naked when you see them, and do not turn your back on your own." — Is 58:6-7

"Come, you who are blessed by My Father! Inherit the Kingdom prepared for you from the foundation of the world. . . . I was sick and you took care of Me."

— Mt 25:34, 36

"We must do the works of Him Who sent Me while it is day. Night is approaching when no one can work."

— Jn 9:4

NOVENA PRAYERS

Novena Prayer

SAINT John of God, I honor you as the patron of the sick, especially of those who are afflicted by heart disease. I choose you to be my patron and protector in my present need. I confidently place before you my earnest petition: *(Mention your request).*

I beg you to recommend my request to Mary, the Mother of Sorrows and Health of the Sick, that both Mary and you may present it to Jesus, the Divine Physician.

Saint John of God, I entrust my soul, my body, all my spiritual and temporal interests to you. To you I entrust my mind, that in all things it may be enlightened by faith, above all in accepting my cross as a blessing from God; my heart, that you may keep it pure and fill it with the love for Jesus and Mary that burned in yours; my will, that like yours, it may always be one with the Will of God.

Saint John of God, I honor you as the model of penitents, for you received the grace to give up a sinful life and to atone for our sins by untiring labors in behalf of the poor and sick. Obtain for me the grace from God to be truly sorry for my sins, to make atonement for them and never again offend God. Aid me in mastering my evil inclinations and temptations, and in avoiding all occasions of sin.

Through your intercession may I obtain the grace from Jesus and Mary to fulfill faithfully all the duties of my state of life and to practice those virtues which are needful for my salvation. Help me to belong to God and Our Lady in life and in death through perfect love. May my life, like yours, be spent in the untiring service of God and my neighbor.

I beg you to be with me in my last hour and pray for me. As you died kneeling before a crucifix, may I find strength, consolation and salvation in the Cross of my Redeemer, and through His tender mercy and the prayers of Our Lady, and through your intercession, attain to eternal life. Amen.

Prayer

GOD, You enabled Saint John, who was inflamed with love of You, to serve the sick, and by him You enriched Your Church with a new religious Order. Grant, through the help of his prayers and merits, that our vices may be healed by the fire of Your love, and that we may receive remedies that will help us reach eternal life. We ask this through Christ our Lord. Amen.

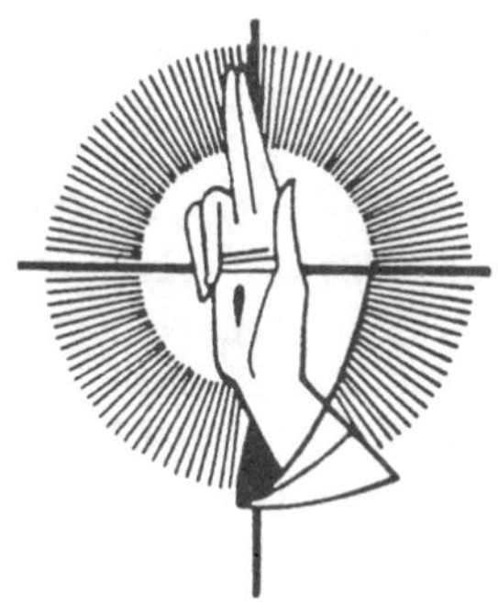

SAINT JOSEPH

(March 19; May 1)

Patron of the Universal Church

MEDITATION

SAINT Joseph is venerated as the husband of the Blessed Virgin Mary, the legal father of Jesus, and the head of the Holy Family. He was Mary's support and protector, a witness to her virginity, a consoler in her difficult vocation.

God comforted Joseph in a prophetic dream. He revealed to him in some measure the mystery of the Incarnation, the adorable Name of Jesus and His mission on earth. He removed every doubt from Joseph's mind and encouraged him to take to himself Mary for his wife. He freed him from worry and rewarded him with honors.

Joseph's sanctity was great to render him worthy of such a vocation. His holiness is measured by his close relation to Mary, his spotless Virgin-Spouse, and to Jesus, his Divine Foster-Child.

His union with Mary is the closest that can exist, a union of heart with heart, a union of purest and holiest love. To what heights of sanctity must he have risen during this holy union on earth!

As the foster-father of Jesus, Joseph stands in close relation to the Son of God, the Fountain of all holiness. He surely has a greater share in his infinite sanctity than any other Saint, excepting Mary. Numberless are the graces and privileges connected with his exalted office.

We should love and honor him whom Jesus and His Mother love so tenderly. Through his intercession we can obtain the grace to love Jesus and Mary with some of that tenderness and devotedness with which he loves them.

Joseph served the Divine Child with a singular love. God gave him a heart filled with heavenly, supernatural love—a love far deeper and more powerful than any natural father's love could be.

Joseph served Jesus with great unselfishness, without any regard to self-interest, but not without sacrifices. He did not toil for himself, but he seemed to be an instrument intended for the benefit of others, to be put aside as soon as it had done its work, for he disappeared from the scene once the childhood of Jesus had passed.

Joseph's is a very special rank among the Saints of the Kingdom of God, because he was so much a part of the very life of the Word of God made Man. In his house at Nazareth and under his care the redemption of mankind was prepared. What he accomplished, he did also for those for whom Jesus was to give His life. He is not only a powerful and great Saint in the Kingdom of God but a benefactor of the whole of Christendom and mankind. His rank in the Kingdom of God, surpassing far in dignity and honor all the Angels and Saints, deserves our very special veneration, love, and gratitude.

THE WORD OF GOD

"Joseph, [Mary's] husband . . . was as just man."
—Mt 1:19

"He holds victory in store for the upright, he is the shield of those who walk blamelessly, for he guards the paths of the just, and protects the way of the pious ones."
— Prv 2:7-8

" 'Joseph, son of David, do not fear to take Mary as your wife. . . . She will have a Son and you are to name Him Jesus because He will save His people from their sins.' . . . When Joseph awoke he did as the Angel of the Lord had commanded him." — Mt 1:20-21, 24

"[Jesus] went down with them and came to Nazareth, and He was obedient to [Mary and Joseph]." — Lk 2:51

NOVENA PRAYERS

Novena Prayer

SAINT Joseph, you are the faithful protector and intercessor of all who love and venerate you. I have special confidence in you. You are powerful with God and will never abandon your faithful servants.

I humbly invoke you and commend myself, with all who are dear to me, to your intercession. By the love you have for Jesus and Mary, do not abandon me during life, and assist me at the hour of my death.

Glorious Saint Joseph, spouse of the immaculate Virgin, Foster-father of Jesus Christ, obtain for me a pure, humble, and charitable mind, and perfect resignation to the Divine Will. Be my guide, my father, and my model through life that I may merit to die as you did in the arms of Jesus and Mary.

Loving Saint Joseph, faithful follower of Jesus Christ, I raise my heart to you to implore your powerful intercession in obtaining from the Heart of Jesus all the graces necessary for my spiritual and temporal welfare, particularly the grace of a happy death, and the special grace I now implore: *(Mention your request).*

Guardian of the Word Incarnate, I am confident that your prayers in my behalf will be graciously heard before the throne of God.

Remember, Saint Joseph

REMEMBER, most pure spouse of Mary, ever Virgin, my loving protector, Saint Joseph, that no one ever had recourse to your protection or asked your aid without obtaining relief.

Confiding, therefore, in your goodness, I come before you and humbly implore you. Despise not my petitions, Foster-father of the Redeemer, but graciously receive them.

Consecration of the Family

JESUS, our most loving Redeemer, You came to enlighten the world with Your teaching and example. You willed to spend the greater part of Your life in humble obedience to Mary and Joseph in the poor home of Nazareth. In this way You sanctified that Family which was to be an example for all Christian families.

Jesus, Mary, Joseph! Graciously accept our family which we dedicate and consecrate to You. Be pleased to protect, guard, and keep it in sincere faith, in peace, and in the harmony of Christian charity. By conforming ourselves to the Divine model of Your Family, may we all attain to eternal happiness.

Mary, Mother of Jesus and our Mother, by your merciful intercession make this our humble offering acceptable to Jesus, and obtain for us graces and blessings.

Saint Joseph, most holy guardian of Jesus and Mary, help us by your prayers in all our spiritual and temporal needs so that we may praise Jesus, our Divine Savior, together with Mary and you for all eternity.

For the Church

GLORIOUS Saint Joseph, powerful protector of Holy Church, I implore your heavenly aid for the whole Church on earth, especially for the Holy Father and all bishops, priests, and religious.

Comfort the afflicted, console the dying, and convert sinners and heretics. Have pity on the poor souls in purgatory, especially on my own family, relatives, and friends. Obtain for them the speedy remission of their punishment, that with you and all the Saints and Angels they may praise and glorify the Blessed Trinity forever.

Prayer

GOD our Father, creator and ruler of the universe, in every age You call human beings to develop and use their gifts for the good of others. With Saint Joseph as our example and guide, help us to do the work You have asked and come to the rewards You have promised.

Inspired by the example of Saint Joseph, may our lives manifest Your love and may we rejoice forever in Your peace. Grant this through Christ our Lord. Amen.

Litany of Saint Joseph

LORD, have mercy.
Christ, have mercy.
Lord, have mercy.
Christ hear us.
Christ, graciously hear us.
God the Father of heaven, *have mercy on us.*
God the Son, Redeemer of the world,*
God the Holy Spirit,
Holy Trinity, one God,
Holy Mary, *pray for us.*
Saint Joseph,**
Renowned offspring of David,
Light of patriarchs,
Spouse of the Mother of God,

* *Have mercy on us* is repeated for these next three invocations.

** *Pray for us* is repeated after each invocation.

Chaste guardian of the Virgin,
Foster-father of the Son of God,
Diligent protector of Christ,
Head of the Holy Family,
Joseph most just,
Joseph most chaste,
Joseph most prudent,
Joseph most strong,
Joseph most obedient,
Joseph most faithful,
Mirror of patience,
Lover of poverty,
Model of artisans,
Glory of home life,
Guardian of virgins,
Pillar of families,
Solace of the wretched,
Hope of the sick,
Patron of the dying,
Terror of demons,
Protector of Holy Church,
Lamb of God, You take away the sins of the world; *spare us, O Lord.*
Lamb of God, You take away the sins of the world; *graciously hear us, O Lord.*
Lamb of God, You take away the sins of the world; *have mercy on us.*
℣. He has made him the lord of His house,
℟. *And the ruler of His possessions.*

Prayer

LET us pray. O God, in Your ineffable providence You were pleased to choose Blessed Joseph to be the spouse of Your most holy Mother. Grant, we beg You, that we may be worthy to have him for our intercessor in heaven whom on earth we venerate as our Protector: You Who live and reign forever and ever. ℟. *Amen.*

— MAY —

SAINT PEREGRINE

(May 2)

Patron of Cancer Patients

MEDITATION

PEREGRINE was born in 1260 at Forli, Italy. He belonged to an anti-papal party. St. Philip Benizi was sent by the Pope to preach peace at Forli. Peregrine knocked down the holy man by striking him on the face. The Saint's only reply was to pray for the youth. This impressed Peregrine, and he begged forgiveness on his knees.

Our Lady appeared to Peregrine and told him to go to Siena, where he was received into the Order of the Servants of Mary by Saint Philip himself.

Peregrine was to have his foot cut off because of a spreading cancer. While spending the night before the operation in prayer, he fell asleep before the image of the crucified Savior. In a dream, Christ seemed to stretch out His hand from the Cross and touch his diseased foot. On awakening he was completely cured.

For sixty-two years Peregrine lived a life of penance and prayer as a saintly priest. He died in 1345. He was chosen by the Church to be the patron of those suffering from running sores and cancer. Four hundred years after burial, the body of "the Cancer Saint" was found to be incorrupt. He is invoked as the patron of cancer patients. His feast is celebrated on May 2.

THE WORD OF GOD

"Through Christ you have been granted the privilege not only to believe in Him but also to suffer for Him."

— Phil 1:29

"You will weep and mourn while the world rejoices; you will be sorrowful, but your grief will be turned into joy."

— Jn 16:20

"By patient endurance you will gain life." — Lk 21:19

NOVENA PRAYERS

Novena Prayer

SAINT Peregrine, whom Holy Mother Church has declared patron of those suffering from running sores and cancer, I confidently turn to you for aid in my present need: *(Mention your request).*

Lest I lose confidence, I beg your kind intercession. Plead with Mary, the Mother of Sorrows, whom you loved so tenderly and in union with whom you have suffered the pains of cancer, that she may help me with her all-powerful prayers and consolation.

Obtain for me the strength to accept my trials from the loving hand of God with patience and resignation. May suffering lead me to a better life and enable me to atone for my own sins and the sins of the world.

Saint Peregrine, help me to imitate you in bearing whatever cross God may permit to come to me, uniting myself with Jesus Crucified and the Mother of Sorrows. I offer my sufferings to God with all the love of my heart, for His glory and the salvation of souls, especially my own. Amen.

Prayer

GOD, graciously hear the prayers which I present to You in honor of Saint Peregrine, Your beloved servant and devoted friend of Jesus Crucified and Our Mother of Sorrows, so that I may receive help in my needs through the intercession of him whose life had been so pleasing to You.

You filled Saint Peregrine with the spirit of compassion. Grant that by practicing works of charity I may deserve to be numbered among the elect in Your Kingdom. I ask this through Christ our Lord. Amen.

SAINT DYMPHNA

(May 15)

Patron of the Nervous and Emotionally Disturbed

MEDITATION

SAINT Dymphna was born in the seventh century. Her father, Damon, a chieftain of great wealth and power, was a pagan. Her mother was a very beautiful and devout Christian.

Dymphna was fourteen when her mother died. Damon is said to have been afflicted with a mental illness, brought on by his grief. He sent messengers throughout his own and other lands to find some woman of noble birth, resembling his wife, who would be willing to marry him. When none could be found his evil advisers told him to marry his own daughter. Dymphna fled from her castle together with Saint Gerebran, her confessor, and two other friends.

Damon found them in Belgium. He gave orders that the priest's head be cut off. Then he tried to persuade his daughter to return to Ireland with him. When she refused, he drew his sword and struck off her head. She was then only fifteen years of age.

Dymphna received the crown of martyrdom in defense of her purity about the year 620. She is the patron of those suffering from nervous and mental afflictions. Many miracles have taken place at her shrine, built on the spot where she was buried in Gheel, Belgium. Her feast is celebrated on May 15.

THE WORD OF GOD

"Those who have believed . . . will expel demons in My Name, . . . and the sick upon whom they lay their hands will recover." — Mk 16:17-18

"He will rescue you from the snare of the hunter, from the destroying pestilence." — Ps 91:3

"They that are planted in the house of the Lord shall prosper in the courts of our God." — Ps 92:14

NOVENA PRAYERS

Novena Prayer

SAINT Dymphna, a great wonderworker in every affliction of mind and body, I humbly implore your powerful intercession with Jesus through Mary, the Health of the Sick.

You are filled with love and compassion for the thousands of patients brought to your shrine for centuries, and for those who cannot come to your shrine but invoke you in their own homes or in hospitals. Show the same love and compassion toward me, your faithful client. The many miracles and cures which have been wrought through your intercession give me great confidence that you will help me in my present need: *(Mention your request).*

I am confident of obtaining my request, if it is for the greater glory of God and the good of my soul. For the sake of Jesus and Mary, whom you loved so earnestly, and for whom you offered your life in martyrdom, grant my prayer.

Saint Dymphna, young and beautiful, innocent and pure, help me to imitate your love of purity. You chose to be martyred by your own father's sword rather than consent to sin. Give me strength and courage in fighting off the temptations of the world and evil desires.

As you have given all the love of your heart to Jesus, help me to love God with my whole heart and serve Him faithfully. As you bore the persecution of your father and the sufferings of an exile so patiently, obtain for me the patience I need to accept the trials of my life with loving resignation to the will of God.

Saint Dymphna, through your glorious martyrdom for the love of Christ, help me to be loyal to my faith and my God as long as I live. And when the hour of my own death comes, stand at my side and pray for me that I may at last merit the eternal crown of glory in God's Kingdom.

Good Saint Dymphna, I beg you to recommend my request to Mary, the Health of the Sick and Comforter of the Afflicted, that both Mary and you may present it to Jesus, the Divine Physician.

Prayer

O GOD, You gave Saint Dymphna to Your Church as a model of all virtues, especially holy purity, and willed that she should seal her faith with her innocent blood and perform numerous miracles. Grant that we who honor her as patroness of those afflicted with nervous and mental illness may continue to enjoy her powerful intercession and protection and attain eternal life. We ask this through Christ our Lord. Amen.

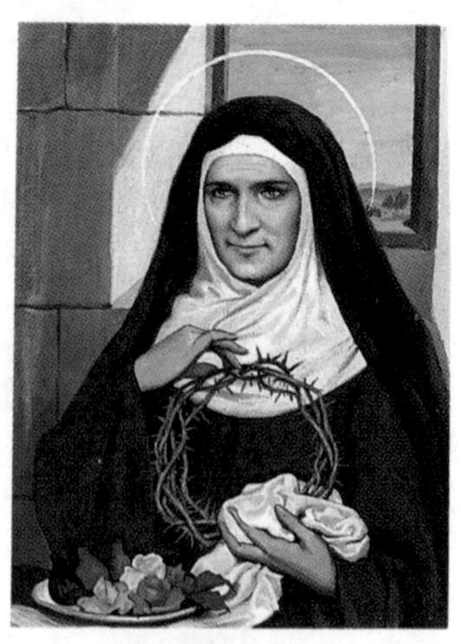

SAINT RITA

(May 22)

Saint of the Impossible

MEDITATION

SAINT Rita might be described as the Saint with family troubles: she was in a very real sense the victim of an unhappy marriage. She was born in 1381 of an ordinary peasant family in central Italy.

When Rita at an early age showed an inclination for convent life and asked permission of her parents to follow that vocation, they would not hear of it. Instead, as Rita reached the age of fifteen, they arranged a marriage for her, according to the custom of that day, with a man of their own choice. And Rita, with a sad heart, yet feeling that to obey her parents in this matter was to obey God, settled down in her new vocation, resolved to be a good wife that thus she might save and sanctify her soul.

Rita's husband was a man of violent temper, which developed into brutality. He often kicked and struck his young wife for no other reason perhaps than that he was angry for losing at gambling. Rita's husband was guilty of open infidelity.

Two sons were born to them in the early years of their married life. Although Rita did her best to train them and educate them to the knowledge and love of God, their father delighted in teaching them his own evil ways.

One night her husband was stabbed by an enemy he made as a result of his violent way of life. Before he died, he came to himself, and showed every sign of repentance for his evil life, which surely was the result of Rita's prayers.

The boys died soon after at a very early age. "Only let them die in Your grace, O Lord," she prayed. Her prayer was heard. Both on their deathbeds had time to repent and to receive the Sacraments.

For eighteen years Rita bore heroically the troubles of her married life. Left alone in the world, she soon sought admission into a nearby Augustinian convent. But her suffering was not ended.

When Rita was about sixty years old, a small wound appeared on her forehead, as though a thorn from Christ's crown of thorns had penetrated her own flesh. For the last sixteen years of life, this mystic of the Cross patiently and lovingly bore that external and painful sign of stigmatization and union with Christ. Since it was accompanied by a wasting sickness, Rita had to be taken care of in an isolated part of her convent.

At last, with perfect resignation to God's Will, she died, on May 22, 1457, acclaimed a Saint by all, and was soon officially declared a Saint by the Church. Her feast is celebrated on May 22.

THE WORD OF GOD

"I have come to set a man against his father, a daughter against her mother. Your enemies will be the members of your own household." — Mt 10:35-36

"As long as you remain in Me and I in you, you bear much fruit, but apart from Me you can do nothing." — Jn 15:5

"I do not wish to boast of anything but the Cross of our Lord Jesus Christ. Through it, the world has been crucified to me and I to the world." — Gal 6:14

NOVENA PRAYERS

Prayer to the Heavenly Father

HEAVENLY Father, rewarder of the humble, You blessed Saint Rita with charity and patience. You kept her faithful to the pattern of poverty and humility of Your Son during the years of her married life and especially in the convent where she served You for the rest of her life.

In Saint Rita You give us an example of the Gospel lived to perfection, for You called her to seek Your Kingdom in this world by striving to live in perfect charity. In her life You teach us that the commandments of heaven are summarized in love of You and love of others.

May the prayers of Saint Rita help me and her example inspire me to carry my cross and to love You always. Pour upon me the spirit of wisdom and love with which You filled Your servant, so that I may serve You faithfully and reach eternal life. I ask this through Christ our Lord. Amen.

Novena Prayer

SAINT Rita, God gave you to us as an example of charity and patience, and offered you a share in the Passion of His Son. I thank Him for the many blessings He bestowed upon you during your lifetime, especially during your unhappy marriage and during the illness you suffered in the convent.

May your example encourage me to carry my own Cross patiently and to live a holier life. By serving God as you did, may I please Him with my faith and my actions.

I fail because of my weakness. Pray to God for me that He may restore me to His love through His grace and help me on my way to salvation.

In your kindness hear my prayer and ask God to grant me this particular request if it be His Will: *(Mention your request).*

May your prayers help me to live in fidelity to my calling as you did and bring me to the deeper love of God and my neighbor until I reach eternal life in heaven. Amen.

Alternative Novena Prayer

HOLY Patroness of those in need, Saint Rita, your pleadings before your Divine Lord are irresistible. For your lavishness in granting favors you have been called the "Advocate of the Hopeless" and even of the "Impossible." You are so humble, so mortified, so patient, and so compassionate in love for your crucified Jesus that you can obtain from Him anything you ask. Therefore, all confidently have recourse to you in the hope of comfort or relief.

Be propitious toward your suppliants and show your power with God in their behalf. Be lavish of your favors now as you have been in so many wonderful cases for the greater glory of God, the spread of your devotion, and the consolation of those who trust in you. We promise, if our petition be granted, to glorify you by making known your favor, and to bless you and sing your praises forever. Relying then on your merits and power before the Sacred Heart of Jesus, we ask of you: *(Mention your request).*

Prayer

O GOD, in Your infinite tenderness You have been pleased to regard the prayer of Your servant Rita, and to grant to her supplication that which is impossible to human foresight, skill, and effort, in reward for her compassionate love and firm reliance on Your promises.

Have pity on our adversities and comfort us in our calamities, that unbelievers may know that You are the recompense of the humble, the defense of the helpless, and the strength of those who trust in You. Grant this in the Name of Jesus the Lord.

— JUNE —

SAINT ANTHONY OF PADUA

(June 13)

The Wonderworker

MEDITATION

ANTHONY'S parents were rich and wanted him to be a great nobleman. But he wanted to be poor for the sake of Christ, so he became a Franciscan.

Anthony was a great preacher. He was sent out as a missionary and preached in many cities in Italy and France. He brought many sinners back to God, mostly by his good example.

It is said that when Anthony was praying in his room, the Infant Jesus appeared to him, put His little arms around his neck, and kissed him. This wonderful favor was given to Anthony because he kept his soul free from even the smallest sin and because he loved Jesus very much.

When Anthony became ill he went to a monastery outside of Padua, where he died at the age of only thirty-six on June 13, 1231. Thirty-two years after his death his remains were brought to Padua. All the flesh except the tongue had been consumed by corruption. Many miracles took place after his death. Even today he is called the "Wonderworker." His feast is celebrated on June 13.

Saint Anthony is one of the most popular of Saints. He is called the "Saint of the Whole World" because the faithful of the whole world love him. During the past seven hundred years, millions have been attracted to this great Franciscan Wonderworker.

Another Franciscan, Saint Bonaventure, says, "Ask the Wonderworker with confidence, and he will obtain what you seek."

THE WORD OF GOD

"The Spirit of the Lord is upon Me. He has anointed Me to bring good news to the poor." — Lk 4:18

"I proclaim Your justice in the great assembly; . . . I have spoken of Your faithfulness and Your salvation."
— Ps 40:10-11

"The just man's tongue is like choice silver. . . . The just man's lips nourish many." — Prv 10:20-21

NOVENA PRAYERS

Novena Prayer

SAINT Anthony, glorious for the fame of your miracles, obtain for me from God's mercy this favor that I desire: *(Mention your request).*

Since you were so gracious to poor sinners, do not regard my lack of virtue but consider the glory of God which will be exalted once more through you by the granting of the petition that I now earnestly present to you.

Glorious Wonderworker, Saint Anthony, father of the poor and comforter of the afflicted, I ask for your help. You have come to my aid with such loving care and have comforted me so generously. I offer you my heartfelt thanks.

Accept this offering of my devotion and love and with it my earnest promise which I now renew, to live always in the love of God and my neighbor. Continue to shield me graciously with your protection, and obtain for me the grace of being able one day to enter the Kingdom of heaven, there to praise with you the everlasting mercies of God. Amen.

Litany of Saint Anthony

(For Private Devotion)

LORD, have mercy.
Christ, have mercy.
Lord, have mercy.
Christ, hear us.
Christ, graciously hear us.
Holy Mary, *pray for us.*
Saint Francis,*
Saint Anthony of Padua,
Glory of the Order of Friars Minor,
Martyr in desiring to die for Christ,
Pillar of the Church,

**Pray for us* is repeated after each invocation down to *Be merciful to us.*

Worthy priest of God,
Apostolic preacher,
Teacher of truth,
Conqueror of heretics,
Terror of evil spirits,
Comforter of the afflicted,
Helper in necessities,
Guide of the erring,
Restorer of lost things,
Chosen intercessor,
Continuous worker of miracles,
Be merciful to us, *spare us, O Lord.*
Be merciful to us, *hear us, O Lord.*
From all evil, *deliver us, O Lord.*
From all sin,**
From all dangers of body and soul,
From the snares of the devil,
From pestilence, famine, and war,
From eternal death,
Through the merits of Saint Anthony,
Through his zeal for the conversion of sinners,
Through his desire for the crown of martyrdom,
Through his fatigues and labors,
Through his preaching and teaching,
Through his penitential tears,
Through his patience and humility,
Through his glorious death,
Through the number of his prodigies,
In the day of judgment,
We sinners, *we beseech You, hear us,*
That You would bring us to true penance,***
That You would grant us patience in our trials,
That You would assist us in our necessities,
That You would hear our prayers and petitions,
That You would kindle the fires of Divine love within us,

** *Deliver us, O Lord* is repeated after each invocation down to *In the day of judgment.*

*** *We beseech you, hear us,* is repeated after each invocation down to *Son of God.*

That You would grant us the protection and intercession of Saint Anthony,

Son of God,

Lamb of God, You take away the sins of the world; *spare us, O Lord.*

Lamb of God, You take away the sins of the world; *graciously hear us, O Lord.*

Lamb of God, You take away the sins of the world; *have mercy on us.*

Christ, hear us.

Christ, graciously hear us.

℣. Pray for us, O blessed Saint Anthony.

℟. *That we may be made worthy of the promises of Christ.*

Prayer

LET us pray. Almighty and eternal God, You glorified Your faithful confessor Anthony with the perpetual gift of working miracles. Grant that what we confidently seek through his merits we may surely receive by his intercession. We ask this in the Name of Jesus the Lord. ℟. *Amen.*

— JULY —

SAINT ANNE

(July 26)

Patroness of Mothers

MEDITATION

THE *dignity* of Saint Anne is great because her daughter was Mary, predestined from all eternity to be the Mother of God, sanctified in her conception, the undefiled Virgin, the Mediatrix of all graces. Her Grandson was the Son of God made Man, the Messiah, the Expected of Nations. Mary is not only the joy and crown, but the foundation for all the glory and power of her mother.

Saint Anne's *sanctity* is so great because of the many graces that God has bestowed upon her. Her very name signifies "grace." God prepared her with magnificent gifts and graces. As the works of God are perfect, it was natural to expect that He should make her a worthy mother of the most pure creature who was superior in sanctity to all creatures and inferior only to God.

Saint Anne was zealous in performing good works and striving for virtue. She loved God sincerely, and was resigned to His holy Will in all sufferings, such as her sterility during twenty years as tradition suggests. As a wife and mother, she was faithful in fulfilling the duties required of her toward her husband and her loving daughter Mary.

The *power* of Saint Anne's intercession is very great. She is not only a Saint and a friend of God but also the grandmother of Jesus according to the flesh.

The Blessed Trinity will grant her petitions: the Father for Whom she bore, nursed, and trained His favored daughter; the Son, to Whom she gave a mother; the Holy Spirit, Whose bride she educated with such great care.

This favored Saint ranks high in merit and glory, near to the Word Incarnate and to His most holy Mother. Certainly, then, Saint Anne has great power with God. The mother of the Queen of heaven, who is all-powerful through her intercession and the Mother of mercy, is likewise full of power and mercy.

We have every reason to choose Saint Anne as our intercessor before God. As grandmother of Jesus Christ, our Brother according to the flesh, she is also our grandmother and loves us, her grandchildren. She loves us with a great love because her Grandson Jesus died for our souls and Mary, her daughter, became our Mother beneath the Cross. She must love us sincerely because of the two Persons whom she loved most in her life, Jesus and Mary. If her love is so great, her intercession is also great. We should, therefore, go to her with great confidence in our needs. This would certainly please Jesus and Mary who loved her so dearly.

The feast of Saint Anne is celebrated on July 26.

THE WORD OF GOD

"[Anna] was continually in the Temple, worshiping day and night." — Lk 2:37

"[She] shall receive a blessing from the Lord, a reward from God [her] Savior." — Ps 24:5

"Blessed are your eyes because they see, and blessed are your ears because they hear. . . . Many Prophets and holy people longed to see what you see but did not see it." — Mt 13:16-17

NOVENA PRAYERS

Novena Prayer

GLORIOUS Saint Anne, I desire to honor you with a special devotion. I choose you, after the Blessed Virgin, as my spiritual mother and protectress. To you I entrust my soul and my body, all my spiritual and temporal interests, as well as those of my family.

To you I consecrate my mind, that in all things it may be enlightened by faith; my heart, that you may keep it pure and fill it with love for Jesus, Mary, Joseph, and yourself; my will, that like yours, it may always be one with the Will of God.

Good Saint Anne, filled with love for those who invoke you and with compassion for those who suffer, I confidently place before you my earnest petition: *(Mention your request).*

I beg you to recommend my petition to your daughter, the Blessed Virgin Mary, that both Mary and you may present it to Jesus. Through your earnest prayers may my request be granted. But if what I ask for should not be according to the Will of God, obtain for me that which will be for the greater benefit of my soul. By the power and the grace with which God has blessed you, extend to me your helping hand.

But most of all, merciful Saint Anne, I beg you to help me to master my evil inclinations and temptations, and to avoid all occasions of sin. Obtain for me the grace of never offending God, of fulfilling faithfully all the duties of my state of life, and of practicing all those virtues that are needful for my salvation.

Like you, may I belong to God in life and in death through perfect love. And after having loved and honored you on earth as a truly devoted child, may I, through your prayers, have the privilege of loving and honoring you in heaven with the Angels and Saints throughout eternity.

Good Saint Anne, mother of her who is our life, our sweetness and our hope, pray to her for me and obtain my request.

Memorare to Saint Anne

REMEMBER, good Saint Anne, whose name means grace and mercy, that never was it known that anyone who fled to your protection, implored your help or sought your intercession, was left unaided.

Inspired with this confidence, I come before you, sinful and sorrowful. Holy mother of the Immaculate Virgin Mary and loving grandmother of the Savior, do not reject my appeal, but hear me and answer my prayer. Amen.

Prayer to Saint Joachim and Saint Anne

GREAT and glorious patriarch, Saint Joachim, and good Saint Anne, what joy is mine when I consider that you were chosen among all God's holy ones to assist in the fulfillment of the mysteries of God, and to enrich our earth with the great Mother of God, Mary most holy. By this singular privilege, you have become most powerful with both the Mother and her Son, so as to be able to obtain for us the graces that are needful to us.

With great confidence I have recourse to your mighty protection, and I commend to you all my needs, both spiritual and temporal, and those of my family. Especially do I entrust to your keeping the particular favor that I desire and look for from your intercession.

And since you were a perfect pattern of the interior life, obtain for me the grace to pray earnestly, and never to set my heart on the passing goods of this life. Give me a lively and enduring love for Jesus and Mary. Obtain for me also a sincere devotion and obedience to Holy Church and the sovereign pontiff who rules over her, in order that I may live and die in faith and hope and perfect charity. Let me ever invoke the holy Names of Jesus and Mary. And may I thus be saved.

Litany in Honor of Saint Anne

(For Private Devotion)

LORD, have mercy.
Christ, have mercy.
Lord, have mercy.
Christ, hear us.
Christ, graciously hear us.
God the Father of heaven, *have mercy on us.*
God, the Son, Redeemer of the world,*
God, the Holy Spirit,
Holy Trinity, one God,
Saint Anne, *pray for us.*
Offspring of the royal race of David,**
Daughter of the Patriarchs,
Faithful spouse of Saint Joachim,
Mother of Mary, the Virgin Mother of God,
Gentle mother of the Queen of heaven,
Grandmother of Our Savior,
Beloved of Jesus, Mary, and Joseph,
Instrument of the Holy Spirit,
Richly endowed with God's grace,
Example of piety and patience in suffering,
Mirror of obedience,
Ideal of pure womanhood,
Protectress of virgins,

* *Have mercy on us* is repeated for these next three invocations.

** *Pray for us* is repeated after each invocation.

Model of Christian mothers,
Protectress of the married,
Guardian of children,
Support of Christian family life,
Help of the Church,
Mother of mercy,
Mother of confidence,
Friend of the poor,
Example of widows,
Health of the sick,
Cure of those who suffer from disease,
Mother of the infirm,
Light of the blind,
Speech of those who cannot speak,
Hearing of the deaf,
Consolation of the afflicted,
Comforter of the oppressed,
Joy of the Angels and Saints,
Refuge of sinners,
Harbor of salvation,
Patroness of a happy death,
Help of all who have recourse to you,
Lamb of God, You take away the sins of the world; *spare us, O Lord.*
Lamb of God, You take away the sins of the world; *graciously hear us, O Lord.*
Lamb of God, You take away the sins of the world; *have mercy on us.*

℣. Pray for us, good Saint Anne.
℟. *That we may be made worthy of the promises of Christ.*

Prayer

LET us pray. Almighty and eternal God, You were pleased to choose Saint Anne to be the mother of the Mother of Your loving Son. Grant, we pray, that we who confidently honor her may through her prayers attain to everlasting life. We ask this through Jesus Christ our Lord. ℟. *Amen.*

— AUGUST —

SAINT ALPHONSUS LIGUORI

(August 1)

Patron of Arthritis Patients

MEDITATION

ALPHONSUS was born near Naples in Italy, in 1696, of a noble Italian family. At nineteen he began to practice law and became one of the leading lawyers in Naples. He never went to the law courts without having first attended Mass. He then made up his mind to become a priest.

Alphonsus preached missions. Large crowds came to hear him. He often visited the sick. He wrote many spiritual books. He organized a community of priests in honor of the Most Holy Redeemer, the Redemptorists, who preach parish missions.

The Pope commanded Alphonsus to become a bishop. During the thirteen years that he was bishop his health was poor. An attack of rheumatism left him a cripple for the rest of his life. His head was so badly bent that his chin pressed against his chest. He suffered intense pain. Arthritis had gripped his wrists and spine. He continued handling details of work from his bed. Because of his arthritic condition he is invoked as the patron of those who suffer with the disease of arthritis.

Alphonsus had a great love for the Blessed Sacrament and Our Lady. He wrote the *Glories of Mary* and *Visits to the Blessed Sacrament.* He was given the title of "Doctor of the Church."

Alphonsus died on August 1, 1787. His feast is celebrated on August 1.

THE WORD OF GOD

"How I love Your law, O Lord! I meditate on it all day long." — Ps 119:97

"Every scribe who is learned in the Kingdom of God is like the head of the household who can bring from his storeroom new treasures as well as old." — Mt 13:52

"[He] is the faithful and wise servant whom the Master has put in charge of His household to dispense food at the proper time." — Mt 24:45

NOVENA PRAYERS

Novena Prayer

GLORIOUS Saint Alphonsus, Bishop and Doctor of the Church, devoted servant of our Lord and loving child of Mary, I invoke you as a Saint in heaven. I give myself to your protection that you may always be my father, my protector, and my guide in the way of holiness and salvation. Aid me in observing the duties of my state of life. Obtain for me great purity of heart and a fervent love of the interior life after your own example.

Great lover of the Blessed Sacrament and the Passion of Jesus Christ, teach me to love Holy Mass and Holy Communion as the source of grace and holiness. Give me a tender devotion to the Passion of my Redeemer.

Promoter of the truth of Christ in your preaching and writing, give me a greater knowledge and appreciation of the Divine truths.

Gentle father of the poor and sinners, help me to imitate your charity toward others in word and deed.

Consoler of the suffering, help me to bear my daily cross patiently in imitation of your own patience in your long and painful illness and to resign myself to the Will of God.

Good Shepherd of the flock of Christ, obtain for me the grace of being a true child of Holy Mother Church.

Saint Alphonsus, I humbly implore your powerful intercession for obtaining from the Heart of Jesus all the graces necessary for my spiritual and temporal welfare. I recommend to you in particular this favor: *(Mention your request).*

I have great confidence in your prayers. I earnestly trust that if it is God's holy Will, my petition will be granted through your intercession for me at the throne of God.

Saint Alphonsus, pray for me and for those I love. I beg of you, by your love for Jesus and Mary, do not abandon us in our needs. May we experience the peace and joy of your holy death. Amen.

Prayer

HEAVENLY Father, You continually build up Your Church by the lives of Your Saints. Give us grace to follow Saint Alphonsus in his loving concern for the salvation of people and so come to share his reward in heaven. Walking in the footsteps of this devoted servant of Yours, may we be consumed with zeal for souls and attain the reward he enjoys in Your Kingdom. We ask this through Christ our Lord. Amen.

— OCTOBER —

SAINT THERESA OF THE CHILD JESUS

(October 1)

Patroness of the Missions

MEDITATION

THERESA was born January 2, 1873, in Alençón, France. Her parents had nine children. Of these, four died in their infancy and five entered the cloister. The father and mother were worthy examples of true Christian parents. Every morning they assisted at Holy Mass; together they received Holy Communion.

To be a spouse of Christ had been Theresa's ardent desire since the early age of three. When she was nine and again when ten years old, she begged to be received into the Carmel of Lisieux. When she completed her fifteenth year, the door of the convent finally opened to her. There the superiors put her virtues to the sharpest test. On January 10, 1889, she was invested with the holy habit and received the name Sister Theresa of the Child Jesus and of the Holy Face. She pronounced her holy vows on September 8, 1890, and gave herself to the practice of the interior life. On the path of spiritual childhood, of love and confidence, she became a great Saint.

Theresa suffered much during her short life, but it was hidden suffering, which she offered out of love for the conversion of sinners and for the sanctification of priests. She writes: "I know of one means only by which to attain perfection: Love! Let us love, since our heart is made for nothing else. I wish to give all to Jesus, since He makes me understand that He alone is perfect happiness. The good God does not need years to accomplish His work of love in a soul. Love can supply for length of years. Jesus, because He is eternal, regards not the time, but only the love."

Shortly before her death Theresa said, "I feel that my mission is about to begin, my mission of bringing others to love our good God as I love Him, and teaching souls my little way of trust and self-surrender. I will spend my heaven in doing good upon earth." Her mission was to teach souls her way of spiritual childhood. She practiced all the virtues of childhood, but those that attracted her above all were the confidence and tender love that little ones show toward their parents. Love, confidence, and self-surrender are the keys to her spiritual life.

On September 30, 1897, Theresa, a true victim of Divine Love, died of tuberculosis, a disease that in her case had assumed a very painful character. A moment before she died the patient sufferer once more made an act of perfect resignation, and with a loving glance at her crucifix, said, "Oh, I love Him! My God, I love You!" She was twenty-four years old when she died.

Saint Theresa was canonized only twenty-eight years after her death. She was declared patroness of the Foreign Missions. She was canonized by her devoted client, Pope Pius XI. The Pontiff said: "That light enkindled a love by which she lived and of which she died, having given nothing to God but love alone and having resolved to save a multitude of souls that they might love God for eternity. Her shower of mystical roses is proof that she has begun her work, and it is our most keen desire that all the faithful should study Saint Theresa so as to copy her example."

Her feast is celebrated on October 1.

THE WORD OF GOD

"Do not rejoice that the spirits are subject to you, but rejoice that your names are inscribed in heaven."

— Lk 10:20

"Unless you change and become like little children, you will not enter the Kingdom of heaven." — Mt 18:3

"Blessed are the meek, for they will inherit the earth."

— Mt 5.5

NOVENA PRAYERS

Novena Prayer

SAINT Theresa of the Child Jesus, during your short life on earth you became a mirror of angelic purity, of love strong as death, and of wholehearted abandonment to God. Now that you rejoice in the reward of your virtue, turn your eyes of mercy upon me, for I put all my confidence in you.

Obtain for me the grace to keep my heart and mind pure and clean like your own, and to abhor sincerely whatever may in any way tarnish the glorious virtue of purity, so dear to our Lord.

Most gracious Little Rose Queen, remember your promises of never letting any request made to you go unanswered, of sending down a shower of roses, and of coming down to earth to do good. Full of confidence in your power with the Sacred Heart, I implore your intercession in my behalf and beg of you to obtain the request I so ardently desire: *(Mention your request).*

Holy "Little Theresa," remember your promise "to do good upon earth" and shower down your "roses" on those who invoke you. Obtain for me from God the graces I hope for from His infinite goodness. Let me feel the power of your prayers in every need. Give me consolation in all the bitterness of this life, and especially at the hour of death, that I may be worthy to share eternal happiness with you in heaven. Amen.

Prayer

FATHER in heaven, through Saint Theresa of the Child Jesus, You desire to remind the world of the merciful love that fills Your Heart and the childlike trust we should have in You. Humbly we thank You for having crowned with such great glory Your ever-faithful child and for giving her wondrous power to bring to You, day by day, innumerable souls who will praise You eternally.

O Lord, You said, "Unless you . . . become like little children, you shall not enter the Kingdom of heaven" (Mt 18:3); grant us, we beg of You, to walk in the footsteps of Your virgin, Saint Theresa, with humility and purity of intention so that we may obtain eternal rewards. You live and reign forever. Amen.

THE HOLY ANGELS

(October 2)

MEDITATION

ANGELS *join us in worship.* The Angels are ministers of the infinitely good God. It is His Will that they aid us in giving Him worship. Angels preside over meetings for worship as is evident from the prayers of the Church. The Liturgy is a participation in that performed by the Angels in heaven. We should join them in giving praise to God. Their ministry consists in inspiring us with faith and love that we may worthily perform our worship. They prepare us inwardly for the reception of the Sacraments, for the Church calls on their aid.

Angels help us against evil. The Angels help us in our warfare against the evil spirit. The New Testament urges us to have faith in God, faith in Christ, and to have recourse to the weapons of God. God sent His Angels to give us the help we need to resist evil. This is their ministry in the work of our salvation, continuing the battle once begun against Lucifer and his rebellious angels. They suggest thoughts contrary to those which the devils suggest and inspire us to turn to God in prayer. Only in heaven will we know how much they have really helped us in our warfare against evil.

The Angels long for our salvation. Since we share with the Angels in the Divine life, and since we are like them the creatures of God in Christ Jesus, they long for our salvation that we may join them in glorifying God and in enjoying the Beatific Vision.

With joy the Angels accept those God-given missions to minister to our sanctification. Victors over demons, they ask but to shield us from the enemies of our souls. We would do well to ask their assistance to repel the temptations of the evil one.

Angels also present our prayers to God by joining their own supplications to our requests. It is, therefore, to our advantage to call upon them, especially in the hour of trial and above all at the hour of death, that they may defend us from the attacks of our enemies and conduct our souls to heaven.

We have a Guardian Angel. Some among the Angels are commissioned with the care of individual souls: these are the Guardian Angels. This is the traditional doctrine of the early writers of the Church, based upon Scriptural texts and supported by solid reasons. It has been confirmed by the Church, as evidenced by the institution of a feast in honor of the Guardian Angels.

The Creator does not abandon creatures when He has made them exist; He sees that they shall have what they need for natural perfection. Christ died for all mankind and merited the means of salvation for all. Angelic assistance is part of God's universal will to save all people.

Angels also pray to God for us. In the lives of the Saints, we see an easy communication with the angelic world based on simple faith in unseen spirits whose love urges them to pray for individuals and communities before the throne of God.

While the immediate focus of the help given by the Angels is spiritual and supernatural, it includes concern for our bodily needs insofar as these pertain to salvation and sanctification.

Since our Guardian Angel keeps us in touch with heaven, we should love and venerate him and pray to him with confidence. He has ever been and is still our devoted friend, ever ready to help us on our way to heaven. In honoring our Guardian Angel we are honoring God Whom our Angel represents on this earth. We are privileged to have so beautiful and so loyal a creature of God as our friend.

THE WORD OF GOD

"I am sending an Angel before you, to keep you safe on the way and bring you to the place I have prepared. Pay attention to him and heed his voice." — Ex 23:20-21

"He has given command about you to His Angels, that they guard you in all your ways. They will bear you up upon their hands, so that you will not dash your foot against a stone." — Ps 91:11-12

"See that you do not look down upon one of these little ones. I assure you, their Angels in heaven constantly behold My Heavenly Father's face." — Mt 18:10

NOVENA PRAYERS

Novena Prayer

HEAVENLY Father, Creator of heaven and earth, I praise and thank You, not only because You have created the visible world but also because You have created the heavens and called the numberless spirits into being. You created them most splendidly, endowing them with power and understanding, and pouring out upon them the riches of Your grace.

I praise and thank You for having showered these blessings upon the good Angels, especially upon my Guardian Angel, and for having rewarded them with eternal glory after the time of their probation. Now they surround Your throne forever, singing jubilantly: Holy, holy, holy, Lord God of hosts! Heaven and earth are full of Your glory. Hosanna in the highest!

Eternal Son of God, I honor You as the King of the Angels. Yet You Yourself were pleased to take their name and office and to dwell among us as the Angel and Messenger of God. You were the faithful Companion and constant Leader of the chosen people. By Your Incarnation You became the Ambassador of our heavenly Father and the Messenger of the great decree of our redemption.

For Your greater glory, loving King of the Angels, I wish to praise and honor Your servants, the Holy Angels, especially my own Guardian Angel. In union with these Holy Angels I adore and revere You as my Savior and my God.

Holy Spirit, Divine Artist, Finger of God's right hand, by Your power and love the hosts of the Angels were brought into being to adore and serve God. They do so with constant fidelity and ready obedience. They carry out Your commands with fervent love and holy zeal. Divine Spirit, You also created us in Your likeness and made of our souls Your living temples.

I thank You for having given us Your Holy Angels to help, protect, and guide us that we may persevere in Your grace throughout life's journey and safely reach our heavenly home. Help me to be attentive to their guidance that I may do Your holy Will perfectly and at the same time find true happiness in this life and in the next.

Most Holy Trinity, Father, Son, and Holy Spirit, in honor of the Holy Angels, I ask You to grant my special request if it be Your holy Will: *(Mention your request).*

Prayer to the Angels

ANGELS and Archangels, Thrones and Dominations, Principalities and Powers, Virtues of the heavens, Cherubim and Seraphim, praise the Lord forever.

Praise the Lord, all you His Angels, who are mighty in strength and who carry out His commands. Praise the Lord, all you His hosts, His servants who do His Will.

Holy Angel who strengthened Jesus Christ our Lord, come and strengthen us also. Come and do not delay!

Prayer to Our Guardian Angel

MY dear Guardian Angel, you were given to me by my merciful God to be the faithful companion of my earthly exile. I honor and love you as my most devoted friend to whom God has entrusted the care of my immortal soul. With all my heart I thank you for your love and constant care of me.

Dearest Angel-friend, I beg you to guard and protect me, a poor sinner. Conduct me on the way of life. Warn me against every occasion of sin, and fill my soul with wholesome thoughts and loving encouragment to practice virtue. Intercede for me that I may share in your burning zeal in God's service and devoted love for His Divine Will.

Forgive me, loving Guardian, for so often disregarding your advice in the past and for ignoring your inspirations. I shall try in the future to obey you willingly and faithfully. You know the value of my soul in the eyes of God. Never permit me to forget that it was redeemed by the Precious Blood of Jesus Christ. Let no stain of evil disfigure the beauty of my soul, nor any sinful thought or deed rob me of my dignity as a child of God. Keep me from scandal that I may never become an occasion of sin to others and thus destroy the work that Christ has wrought in their souls by His bitter Passion and Death.

Dear Guardian Angel, may I enjoy your protection in this dangerous journey through life that I may reach my eternal home in heaven, there to praise the mercy of God toward me in union with you and all the other Angels and Saints forever. Amen.

Prayer

GOD, in Your Providence You were pleased to send Your Holy Angels to keep watch over us. Grant that we may always be defended and shielded by them and rejoice in their companionship.

Lord, we pray You to visit our home and drive far from it all snares of the enemy. Let Your Holy Angels dwell in it to preserve us in peace. Let Your blessing be always upon us.

Almighty and Everlasting God, in Your loving Providence, You have appointed for all the faithful from their birth a special Angel to be Guardian of their body and soul. Grant that I may so love and honor him whom You have given me, that, protected by Your grace and his help, I may merit to behold, with him and all the angelic host, the glory of Your face in the heavenly Kingdom. You live and reign forever. Amen.

SAINT JUDE THADDEUS

Apostle of Those in Need

(October 28)

MEDITATION

SAINT Jude Thaddeus was closely associated with our Lord by blood relationship through Saints Joachim and Anne, the parents of the Blessed Virgin. A grand-nephew of these two saints, he is at once a nephew of Mary and Joseph, which places him in the relationship of cousin of our Lord.

Jude is the brother of the Apostle James the Less. He had two other brothers, whom the Gospel calls "brethren" of Jesus. When our Lord came back from Judea to Nazareth, he began to teach in the synagogue. The people who heard Him were astonished and said, "Where did this man get this wisdom and these miraculous powers? Isn't this the carpenter's Son? Isn't Mary known to be His mother and aren't James, Joseph, Simon, and [Jude] His brothers?" (Mt 13:54).

The word "brethren" or "brothers" in the Hebrew language usually suggests a near relationship. Jude's father was Clopas. His mother's name was Mary. She was a near relative of the Blessed Virgin. She stood beneath the Cross when Jesus died. "Near the Cross of Jesus stood His Mother, His Mother's sister, Mary the wife of Clopas, and Mary Magdalene" (Jn 19:25).

In his boyhood and youth Jude must have associated with Jesus. At the beginning of the public life of Jesus, Jude left all to follow the Master. As an Apostle, he labored with great zeal for the conversion of the Gentiles. For ten years he worked as a missionary in the whole of Mesopotamia. He returned to Jerusalem for the Council of the Apostles. Later he joined Simon in Libya, where the two Apostles preached the Gospel to the barbarian inhabitants.

Tradition says that he and Simon suffered martyrdom at Suanis, a city of Persia, where they had labored as missionaries. Jude was beaten to death with a club; hence he is represented with a club in his hand. His head was then severed from his body with an ax. His body was brought to Rome and his relics are now venerated in Saint Peter's Basilica.

Saint Jude is known mainly as the author of the New Testament Epistle of Jude. This letter was probably written before the fall of Jerusalem, between the years 62 and 65. In his letter Jude denounces the heresies of that early time and warns the Christians against the seduction of false teaching. He speaks of the judgment to come upon the heretics who are living evil lives and condemns the worldly-minded, the lustful, and "those who cultivate people for the sake of gain." He encourages Christians to remain steadfast in the faith and foretells that false teachers, leading wicked lives and ridiculing religion, will arise, but that they will be punished.

To the pride of the wicked he opposes the humble loyalty of the Archangel Michael. He encourages the Christians to build a spiritual edifice by living lives founded upon faith, love of God, hope, and prayer. He encourages the practice of love of neighbor; he urges Christians to endeavor to convert the heretics by the virtues of their lives.

Jude concludes the letter with a prayer praising God for the Incarnation, by means of which the eternal Word of God, Jesus Christ, took upon Himself our human nature and redeemed mankind.

The feast of Saints Simon and Jude is celebrated on October 28.

THE WORD OF GOD

"Amen, amen, I say to you, whoever has faith in Me will do the works I do, and far greater than these."

— Jn 14:12

"Isn't this the carpenter's Son? Isn't Mary known to be His Mother and aren't James, Joseph, Simon, and [Jude] His brothers?"

— Mt 13:54

"Grow strong in your most holy faith and pray in the Holy Spirit. Persevere in God's love and as you wait for the mercy of our Lord Jesus Christ that leads to eternal life."

— Jude 20-21

NOVENA PRAYERS

Novena Prayer

GLORIOUS Saint Jude Thaddeus, by those sublime privileges with which you were adorned in your lifetime, namely, your relationship with our Lord Jesus Christ according to the flesh, and your vocation to be an Apostle, and by that glory which now is yours in heaven as the reward of your apostolic labors and your martyrdom, obtain for me from the Giver of every good and perfect gift all the graces of which I stand in need: *(Mention your request).*

May I treasure up in my heart the divinely inspired doctrines that you have given us in your Epistle: to build my edifice of holiness upon our most holy faith, by praying for the grace of the Holy Spirit; to keep myself in the love of God, looking for the mercy of Jesus Christ unto eternal life; to strive by all means to help those who go astray.

May I thus praise the glory and majesty, the dominion and power of Him Who is able to keep me without sin and to present me spotless with great joy at the coming of our Divine Savior, the Lord Jesus Christ. Amen.

Consecration to Saint Jude

SAINT Jude, Apostle of Christ and glorious martyr, I desire to honor you with a special devotion. I choose you as my patron and protector. To you I entrust my soul and my body, all my spiritual and temporal interests, as well as those of my family. To you I consecrate my mind so that in all things it may be enlightened by faith; my heart so that you may keep it pure and fill it with love for Jesus and Mary; my will so that, like yours, it may always be one with the Will of God.

I beg you to help me to master my evil inclinations and temptations and to avoid all occasions of sin. Obtain for me the grace of never offending God, of fulfilling faithfully all the duties of my state of life, and of practicing all those virtues that are needful for my salvation.

Pray for me, my holy patron and helper, so that, being inspired by your example and assisted by your prayers, I may live a holy life, die a happy death, and attain to the glory of heaven, there to love and thank God forever. Amen.

Prayer

O GOD, You made Your Name known to us through the Apostles. By the intercession of Saint Jude, let Your Church continue to grow with an increased number of believers. Grant this through Christ our Lord. Amen.

— NOVEMBER —

OUR PATRON SAINT

(All Saints, November 1)

MEDITATION

A PATRON Saint or Blessed is one who, since early Christian times, has been chosen as a special intercessor with God for a particular person, place, community, or organization. The custom arose from the Biblical fact that a change of personal name indicated a change in the person, e.g., Abram to Abraham, Simon to Peter, Saul to Paul; and from the practice of having churches built over the tombs of Martyrs.

At Baptism and Confirmation we have received the name of a Saint whom we should imitate and whose intercession we should invoke. We should frequently pray to our Patron Saint for the needs of soul and body, especially on the Saint's feast day. We can honor our Patron Saint by making a novena in his or her honor.

THE WORD OF GOD

"[O Lord,] with Your Blood You have purchased for God persons from every race and tongue, people and nation. You made of them a Kingdom, and priests to serve our God, and they will reign on the earth." — Rv 5:9-10

"You are the temple of the living God, just as God has said: I will dwell with them and walk among them. I will be their God and they will be My people." — 2 Cor 6:16

"Be holy yourselves in all you do, after the likeness of the Holy One Who called you; for it is written, 'Be holy, for I am holy.' " — 1 Pt 1:15-16

NOVENA PRAYERS

Novena Prayer

GREAT Saint N., at my Baptism you were chosen as a guardian and witness of my obligations, and under your name I then became an adopted child of God, and solemnly renounced Satan, his works, and his empty promises. Assist me by your powerful intercession in the fulfillment of these sacred promises. You also made them in the days of your earthly pilgrimage, and your fidelity in keeping them to the end has obtained for you an everlasting reward in heaven.

I am called to the same happiness that you enjoy. The same help is offered to me that enabled you to acquire eternal glory. You overcame temptations like those that I experience.

Pray for me, therefore, my Holy Patron, so that, being inspired by your example and assisted by your prayers, I may live a holy life, die a happy death, and reach eternal life to praise and thank God in heaven with you.

I ask you to pray to God for this special request if it be God's holy Will: *(Mention your request).*

Prayer

ALMIGHTY, eternal God, You were pleased to make Your Church illustrious through the varied splendor of the Saints. As we venerate their memory may we also follow such shining examples of virtue on earth and thus obtain merited crowns in heaven. We ask this through Christ our Lord. Amen.